SARAH K. HOWLEY

HOPE

A BIBLE STUDY OF
WOMEN IN JESUS' LINEAGE

Hope: A Bible Study of Women in Jesus' Lineage

Flaming Dove Press
an imprint of
InspiritEncourage LLC
1520 Belle View Blvd #5081
Alexandria, VA 22307
www.inspiritencourage.com

ISBN 978-1-960793-10-2 (e-pub)
ISBN 978-1-960793-22-5 (paperback)
ISBN 978-1-960793-23-2 (large print)

Printed in the United States of America

Library of Congress Control Number: 2024903737

Contents

Introduction   1

Week 1: Tamar

    Context   7

    Issue   11

    Action   15

    Blessing   19

    Reflection   23

Week 2: Rahab

    Context   27

    Issue   31

    Action   35

    Blessing   39

    Reflection   43

Week 3: Ruth

    Context   47

    Issues   51

    Action   55

    Blessing   61

    Reflection   65

Week 4: Bathsheba

Context 69

Issue 73

Action 77

Blessing 81

Reflection 85

Conclusion 87

Hope Study Resources 89

Also By Sarah K. Howley 91

About the Author 93

Endnotes 95

Introduction

On the first page of the New Testament in the Bible is a list of names, and I have often been tempted to skip over them, not really connecting names to their actions and significance. It didn't really make sense to me why the opening pages of the greatest story ever told contain a list of names, a genealogy. I used to give this passage in the beginning of Matthew maybe a cursory glance, and then I'd move on to the angels and the shepherds and the birth of Jesus.

However, we need to stop at Matthew 1, knowing that everything God has included in Scripture is intentionally there, *"useful for teaching, rebuking, correcting, and training in righteousness"* (2 Timothy 3:16). To demonstrate the word "correction," I found one image of someone finding the right adjustment to their vision; they were being fitted with glasses. God corrects our understanding of things. And he has recently altered my understanding of these names, making me look at them as people and seeking to know them.

So, let's stop for a moment and take the time to read the beginning of the New Testament.

Read Matthew 1:1-17.

This chapter presents the lineage of Joseph, the earthly father of Jesus. Mainly we see how one man had a son who had a son, who had a son, and so on. I'm sure at some point I was told there are a few women as well in this list. Yet recently God pushed me to focus a bit more on this list. Why does a list of (mostly) men also include four women? What about them elevated them to be included in this list of Jesus' ancestors? In the middle of a list that traces the men of Christ's lineage, we see these four women:

Tamar. Rahab. Ruth. Bathsheba.

I began to look into their stories and see them. You may or may not recall their stories. Ruth's account is a favorite of mine, but I have only recently understood Tamar's story in the right time, place, and lineage. I have studied the stories of Bathsheba and Rahab in the context of the history of Israel, but not the women themselves. Who were they and what did they do? God has fit me with new glasses or lenses in understanding these women.

These four women were all important, which we know because they are included in the lineage of Jesus in the very beginning of Matthew's gospel, the first pages of the New Testament. They were strong women. They faced terrible adversity and mistreatment, and they overcame it to become noted ancestors of Jesus.

I found that each of these women showed great courage and hope. They demonstrated hope that grounds faith.

Hebrews 11:1 defines faith as *"confidence in what we hope for and assurance about what we do not see,"* and then provides examples to help us understand. Noah was told of something unseen and acted by faith. Abraham as well was told of an inheritance in the future, and he went to claim it by faith. And Sarah, who hoped for children, acted in faith to have one. So, we find that faith comes from hope, or rather, we find that hope leads to faith. We see the promise of the future (hope) and are confident in expecting it (faith), and so act. That action is faith expressed and made complete, as James 2:14-26 describes. So, we find that hope is the driver of actions of faith.

Hope that drives our actions of faith could be illustrated as a child who decides she wants to be a doctor when she grows up (or a teacher, virtual assistant, lawyer, or scientist). She doesn't only think, "I hope I will be a doctor one day." She takes steps to get herself there: She studies hard, she joins others to study together, she gets a part-time job in the industry, she reads books outside of school that talk about being a doctor, and she keeps up with the current research in her field of interest. She signs up for pre-med classes and even asks for tutoring when things don't make sense. She actively seeks to achieve what she hopes. She acts in faith to become a doctor.

God Gives Us Hope

Hope is found throughout the Bible. The idea of the future being better than or different from the present only scratches the surface of the biblical definition of hope. There is a certainty or expectation of the fulfillment of that future in biblical hope. The Bible uses three particular words in the original languages to describe hope.

In the Old Testament, written in Hebrew, we find two words: *yakhal* and *qavah*. These words provide a sense of waiting with patience and trust, in the knowledge that God is working. *Qavah* offers an additional sense of tension in hope; the word is more literally translated as "lying in wait."

The idea of hope that we may form with these ideas is similar to the anticipation of hearing the garage door come up and knowing that the only person who has the power (remote) to open that door is the one we love. And that one will come and be good to us and bring us happiness. This is the glancing at the clock as six p.m. draws near, and we know that person is coming. We know even though we have not seen them out the window. We know because of the consistent past, a history of faithfulness to timing, to their word. We wait with tense expectation for this activity; this is hope.

We translate as hope the New Testament Greek word, *elpis*. This word describes an expectation which is certain. The strength of the word "certain" helps solidify the idea that hope is rock solid. In everyday life, we may hear the word hope used as a synonym with the word "wish," but the certainty in biblical hope means that they are different. Our hope is not the hope of the world, which is more of a wish or good thought for something positive. We have perhaps heard there are no guarantees in life, that even gravity may fail. Yet *elpis* challenges all of those little statements about nothing being certain in life. In Christ, much is certain. Starting with him, as the foundation of our biblical hope. We hope in who and not what will happen.

In the brokenness that each of us has experienced, is experiencing, and will experience, it is the presence of God himself that fills us with the hope to carry on. Hope in Christ is knowing that he will act to bring forth his goodness.

We know in our hearts and with all confidence and surety that God will act in the place where we are, the circumstance we are in, and bring light to it.

And perhaps if you are not certain in this "knowing," then this study will help you dig into the hope that is Christ.

These women were not wallflowers; they sought and even fought for their own rights and were blessed. They were commended for their courage and strength. They each had a different vision for their lives than the one they started in; that vision was one of hope that led to heroic actions of faith.

These stories are not all roses and sunshine. These women lived the hard realities of the sin-filled world that we too live in. Abandonment, rape, messy families, uncomfortable situations, sticky, ugly. But God. There was brokenness in their lives, but God redeemed. He redeemed their stories, and their futures. They did not hope in vain but lived in the surety of the unseen. They acted in faith based on hope, and God met them where they were.

This is a study of hope, biblical hope. What it is and what it means for us as followers of Christ, children of God. We will look at the situation that each of the women lived in, what their hope was, and the issues that kept them from realizing that hope. We will see how they acted in faith and were blessed for their godly actions.

Tamar, Rahab, Ruth, and Bathsheba.

TAMAR

Context

Week 1, Day 1 Tamar

We begin our look at women of hope with Tamar. She is the first of the women listed in the Matthew genealogy and the first in order of our Bibles. Her story comes at the time just at the end of the patriarchs Abraham, Isaac, and Jacob, and falls in with the children of Jacob. Her father-in-law is Judah, one of Jacob's sons. Judah left his clan, which was unusual at the time. No explanation was given; we only know that during that time, it was traditional to stay within family and clan during a person's whole life. This provided protection and passed on tradition. However, Judah had gone away and was living in the land of Canaan, where he found his wife and had three sons.

Once the oldest son was of marrying age, Judah *"got a wife for Er"* (Genesis 38:6). At the time of Tamar, a man would usually marry a woman from among his own people, often chosen by his parents and arranged with her family. It is possible that Tamar was asked her opinion, but likely it was a formality rather than actual permission that she gave. Upon marriage, she would have gone to become part of her husband's family and lived in a multi-generational house.

Few details about Tamar are given to us. Since she was living in Canaan, we assume that she was a pagan or at least from outside the Israelite clan. She likely would not have known God of the Israelites and married into a mixed-ethnicity or mixed-religion home, as her mother-in-law was also from the same area. It is never clear if Tamar accepted God or not.

Read Tamar's story in Genesis 38:1-11 and Matthew 1:3.

What were the names of Tamar's first and second husbands? What happened to them and why?

What was Tamar told to do after this happened twice?

The traditional role for women was as daughter, wife, and mother in the times of Tamar. There is evidence that women also ran businesses and were an active part of civil governance; however, they were still expected to marry, have children, and raise them. It was a patriarchal society, so the home was governed by the men, and Tamar would have been cared for first by her father, then her husband, then by her children. Since she and Er had no children, Judah asked Onan to have a child with Tamar, which would be raised as Er's heir.

Onan likely understood that he could take the inheritance if he just never produced an heir for his brother, so it seems that his greed drove him to be wicked as well. And he experienced the consequences for it. This left Tamar without a male heir to care for her. The text tells us that Judah worried his youngest son would end up dead as well if he married Tamar, blaming her for the actions of the first two sons and their consequences. Though Judah promised Tamar his youngest son, Shelah, he sent her to her father's house where she was to wait for him to come of age.

Tamar's Hope

When Tamar married, her hope, or the hope of women of the time, was to be a wife and mother. We can perhaps safely say that Tamar was a wife for several months or years, yet hadn't become a mother. She was sent back to her father and had not seen the hope of becoming a mother realized. She continued to sit with that hope. Her hope and right as a woman at the time was to marry and have a child. Tamar was married into a family who took her in but apparently did not make her part of the family. By sending her back to her family of origin, it was implied the new part of her identity as wife was no longer valid or important.

When we speak of hope, it is important to remember the biblical definition not only of having a better future than present, but that we are certain of it. We have the privilege of knowing the God of hope who works in love and showers us with goodness. He meets us in our waiting and encourages us to lean into him as we hope. At times, our dreams can also be our hopes, but they must be based in God and something that he has placed in our hearts.

Tamar likely did not have this certainty in her hope, since it was not clear from the Bible that she knew God as Judah did. Perhaps Tamar's hope was more a wish for her, a desire to fit in or fulfill other's expectations. We may think "she dreamed of becoming a wife and mother." Yet, as Christians, we have the opportunity to be grounded in certainty about our hope.

Take a moment to consider the things that you look for in the future, how they may be different or better than today. Note down what those hopes are and consider if they are grounded in certainty or if they are more wishes or dreams.

Issue

Week 1, Day 2 Tamar

Tamar was a woman who had lived in her father's household, then her husbands' household, for some time. Then she was sent back to her father's house to wait for Judah's third son, Shelah, to grow up and marry her. She seems to have been passed back and forth. This put her in a situation that none of us want to experience: being alone and unwanted.

The expectations of society would have been such that Tamar "should" have had children since she had been married twice. Society viewed this as a lack, and her being childless would have led to public disgrace. Unfortunately, the disgrace did not end there. Judah had not sent her home to find another husband; he retained his right to find her one. Society would have expected that Tamar's father would have found her a husband and been under his protection and provision when she was sent home. However, this was not the case. She was waiting on her brother-in-law to grow up. This situation implies that Judah did not take his responsibility as the head of household seriously. Judah should have given Tamar the respect of returning to her father's house and being released to remarry, or at the very least, officially betrothed her to her future husband. Instead, Tamar was disgraced in society by not being able to remarry.

Read more of Tamar's story in Genesis 38:11-14.

How much time passed from the death of Tamar's second husband to the time she went to the road at Timnah?

What had happened in Judah's family during the time that had passed?

Tamar found that she was in a time of waiting. She was not released from her husband's family yet was not brought into his family either. As each year passed, Tamar would have known how old Shelah was. Eventually, Tamar knew that the third son was old enough to marry, yet she was not called back from her father's house to marry him. She continued to wait for her father-in-law to agree to the marriage with his youngest son.

Think of a time when you have waited with expectation. Write it down.

Tamar waited in part because of Israelite tradition. The marriage that Tamar waited for has come to be called levirate marriage, levirate meaning "husband's brother," since she was widowed and promised to her husband's brother. This biblical law stated that a brother should produce an heir for the one who died by taking his brother's wife for himself. There is some thought that the law was ideated here in Judah's instructions to his sons and Tamar. The time of Tamar's story is approximately three hundred years before the law was given to the people of Israel by God

(Deuteronomy 25:5-10). At this point, it was only tradition and not a law. It seems from reading the text that Judah may have considered breaking the tradition when his two sons died.

Tamar was sent to her father's home and apparently not betrothed. Her wants, needs, hopes, and desires were not presented within the passage. We can imagine that her hope was to be a wife and mother, but instead, she was left alone and unable to remarry. She was minimized by her father-in-law. Tamar had an issue that was keeping her hope from being realized. She was stuck on hold.

In much of the Old Testament, people asked God for his opinion through a prophet. However, at this time, there were no prophets. This was a post-flood story where prophets had not yet been established. We do not know if Tamar knew God or if Judah introduced his family to God, but she didn't have this option to seek out a prophet of her father-in-law's religion to resolve the issue.

Tamar finds herself in a difficult situation. She did not necessarily have the joy of knowing the Lord to keep her company in her waiting. We are not told that she was a skilled worker who could begin a business to care for herself. We do not know what she did other than return to her father's house. She may have seen more hopelessness than hope. We can only wonder if she prayed to God or took care of household chores. When we hope, or wait with expectation, we have the certainty that God stands with us, and works for our good.

How does knowing God change hopelessness into hope?

When you hope in the Lord, what do you do (or what can you do) to stand firm for such a long time?

As followers of Christ, we are blessed to know that God is with us always as we wait and that he is working in the waiting. I hope that was Tamar's case as well—that God was with her.

Action

Week 1, Day 3 Tamar

Tamar waited for "a long time." Though we do not know exactly how long that was, Tamar stopped waiting at some point and acted on her hope. She had lived as a widow and had done everything in an upstanding manner as far as we are told. She needed to speak to her father-in-law so that she could leave the limbo of living as a widow. She was in-between because she did not have a family, and she could not marry because she had not been released by her father-in-law.

Read Genesis 38:13-23 about when Tamar stopped waiting.

What did Tamar do when she heard her father-in-law was coming to Timnah?

How did Judah respond to seeing Tamar?

What did she request as collateral for her "services"?

It is difficult to understand how Tamar gathered the courage to seek out her father-in-law. She must have considered all her options as she washed the dishes, hung the laundry, and scrubbed the floors. Was it always on her mind, just as so often our concerns and worries are in the forefront? We aren't told.

What do you think made her stop waiting?

What strikes me is how unusual this situation is. The more times I loop back to the "solution" for Tamar's situation, the more outrageous it is to think that she made a plan to prostitute herself to her father-in-law. Most commentaries or lessons describe Tamar as devious and having planned this whole episode, and it seems the veil is the reason for this thought. Yet, when we look into the veil and its use, the earliest evidence of the use of a veil in the Bible is in Genesis 24:65, when a woman meets her future husband and it was used for modesty.[1] Research into ancient customs of the geographic area suggests that only mothers, daughters, and widows veiled themselves in public and prostitutes and servants were unveiled.[2] Perhaps Judah interpreted something that Tamar didn't intend.

In the end, we do not have absolute certainty over the use of a veil, and if the veil was used by prostitutes, it may have been the only way for Tamar to be on the streets alone. At that time, women went out in groups for safety, so her approach may have only been possible by pretending to be a prostitute or by trying to cover or hide herself. For whichever reason she wore a veil, she risked her life on the streets alone to realize her hope.

Perhaps there was not a plan of action before she approached Judah on the road. She may have veiled herself to get close and see if she could find a way to talk to him. In talking to him, perhaps she would have just opened with a request to release her so she may marry and not worry about the time when her father passed away and no one was responsible for caring for her. Perhaps she was surprised to be propositioned by her father-in-law, not expecting it from him. And perhaps many of those commentators are correct and she wanted to make Judah take his responsibility for her by trapping him. We cannot know her motives or thoughts at the time since we are not given them in the passage.

Whatever Tamar's plan was for that roadside encounter, we only know what actually occurred. She slept with a man who was not her husband. By doing so, she accepted the risk of adding to her the public scandal, potentially becoming pregnant while still an unmarried widow.

> Do you believe Tamar's actions were justified? Why or why not?

We also know that she asked for three items in pledge for her "payment": his seal and its cord, and his staff (Genesis 38:18). These three items together show us something of Judah. The seal was used to mark and authenticate documents; they were often carved of stone and engraved with the owner's symbol. These were valuable items in their use, but rather small and worn on a cord. The cord may have been a small tassel as on a belt or a longer cord worn on the neck, but together with the seal, they were the equivalent of today's identity card. The staff that he gave up was representative of his authority and leadership in the family and community. A staff was unique to the person and well-known to the owner as well as those in their sphere of influence.

Tamar audaciously asked for three items which would identify Judah, and he handed over these significant items to a woman he thought he didn't know. Her identity as a member of his family had been taken when she was sent back to her father's house, yet she was also unable to establish a new identity for herself when he didn't release her. It's ironic that she then held his identity in her hands.

This may be a good moment to remind ourselves that the Bible is the story of God and man's response to him. The Bible is not an account of man's (or woman's) righteousness in God's eyes. The actions of the men and women of the Bible are not always guided by God himself, nor ordained as correct, good, and repeatable. Tamar did not act in a way we should emulate. Rather, what we have is the story of how God continues to love us and be our hope, even as we make choices that he may not have wanted.

Tamar was perhaps struggling with gaining her right to a family and God may have supported her hope being realized, but he likely was not happy to see how Judah and Tamar behaved to realize that hope. Yet, God is faithful even when we act in ways that are displeasing.

Are there choices that you have made that God may not have been pleased with, but he saw past your actions to your heart? Jot them here and note how God was faithful in your situation.

Blessing

Week 1, Day 4 Tamar

Tamar approached Judah, though we do not know her motive for doing so. She obtained three items which could be used to identify him and apparently did not reveal her own identity. She held Judah's identity in her hands, as well as a symbol of his leadership. Tamar went home and continued to wait for her hope to be realized, to move out of waiting and into a different future.

Read the remainder of Tamar's story in Genesis 38:24-30.

Who pronounced judgment on Tamar?

How was Tamar saved from being burned?

What do the names of Tamar's children mean?

Tamar became pregnant and gave birth to two sons. Her hope was to have her rights to motherhood restored, and it did happen. God may not have agreed with the way that things came about, but he supported justice in her situation. The re-establishment of Tamar's rights and the chastisement of Judah's behavior brought about the realization of Tamar's hope. Tamar's hope to be a wife, according to the passage, was not realized. By not laying with Judah again, it would seem that she remained a widow.

Judah had minimized Tamar's identity by leaving her a widow though his son had come of age, and he had ill-used his authority over the family when he did not fulfill his promise of marriage. Yet we see the acknowledgement of his lack of righteousness when Tamar cleverly reveals his sin along with hers by sending the collateral to him. Tamar held the items which symbolized his identity and authority; through them, she re-established her identity and God's authority over their lives. God re-established her rights to a child and her first husband's rights to an heir.

Tamar will forever be identified as an ancestor of Jesus Christ. Her right to a child was re-established and through that, her identity will be forever remembered. She brought forth the line of Judah which includes Jesus, our savior. Tamar is a matriarch of the Old Testament.

Tamar waited for long enough and then took steps to secure her future. Because our hope is in Christ, it is for something. She watched out for her future husband and knew he was of age, but she was not called to his side. She watched out for her husband's family and saw that her father-in-law was widowed, single again. She was more righteous in approaching him in hiding than he was in withholding his son. Not that she was right—it wasn't an absolute, but a comparison. We do our best as we (sometimes blindly) go forward and expect God to show up in his goodness and guidance.

Tamar made the tough choices to do what she felt was right. She may not have known how those choices were going to turn out, but what we see in this account is that she risked, and God was with her. She risked much—the position in her father's house as well as her father-in-law's house, her very life—to gain the respect and honor that she never should have lost.

And, Judah stated, *"she is more righteous than I,"* (Genesis 38:26). Please note it says "more righteous," not "unconditionally righteous." The comparison is not an absolute. Neither one of them was righteous, but rather, one was bad, and one was "less bad," so to speak. Tamar was "more righteous" since she approached him to do the right thing by her.

But where was God in all this? I have to ask. That question is helpful to ask whenever we read the Bible. It is the book about the chase that God gives his people out of love. He is chasing us. But the accounts always include the messiness of our lives. He chases and we mess up. And, amazingly, he keeps loving and chasing us.

What we see is God's faithfulness to Tamar's intention of heart despite the sin that was involved. It doesn't seem that anyone sought God's direction here, so how does God show up?

Take a moment to consider what events indicate that God was active and vibrant in the lives of Tamar and Judah, even if we were not told they were seeking him. Note those events that demonstrate God's involvement here.

How have you seen God active in your own life, even in times when you were not seeking him or did not yet call him "Lord"?

Reflection

Week 1, Day 5 Tamar

Hope in God doesn't guarantee things will happen the way we want them; it guarantees that God will act in goodness to provide. Often, we hope in such a way that the entire journey is mapped out instead of hoping in the end result. Tamar's journey to becoming a mother was convoluted, painful, and lonely. It was filled with wrongs done to her.

Tamar's rights were taken from her and the person in authority over her ill-used it. What does the account tell us of how God views this kind of mistreatment?

What does Tamar's account tell us of how God views women?

Have you seen or experienced mistreatment of rights and authority? Describe it and provide a hopeful vision of what will come.

Despite the mistreatment of Tamar, we see through God's blessings that he was present in the life of Tamar. God was there. God is involved with all of his creation, and that means that he is present even if Tamar didn't know him personally. He is always with us, never leaves us, and he gives us hope and a future.

In Jeremiah 29:11, we are reminded of God's presence and intentions for our good. The Israelites were in exile, and those in Jerusalem were told they would suffer mistreatment of the sword, famine, and plague, yet God said that he had plans for their goodness.

'For I know the plans I have for you,' declares the Lord, 'plans to prosper you and not to harm you, plans to give you hope and a future.'

Even though we experience pain and are wronged, God is with us and plans for our hope and our future.

How does Tamar's account remind you that God works for your future?

RAHAB

Context

Week 2, Day 1 Rahab

Rahab appears in the biblical timeline several generations after Tamar. She lived in the Canaanite city of Jericho at the time when the Israelites had been wandering the desert with Moses, who had just passed away. One of the first objectives of Joshua, Moses' successor, was to lead God's people into the promised land. The previous time in the Bible when people had gone to scope out the land that God had promised them, the majority of the group returned in fear of the people in the land. They had described it as a land of strong people with large, fortified cities, and they were not certain in taking the land as God had told them to do. They were then barred from entering the promised land so that a new generation of faithful would enter rather than those who did not believe.

To prepare for entering this land, the first city this new faithful generation would encounter was Jericho, and Joshua sent spies to report the conditions they found there. By this time, forty years had passed, and no update during that time was recorded in the Bible. The two spies Joshua sent landed at Rahab's door; she was a prostitute who lived on the outer edges of the city, at or in the city wall.

There is some discussion among theologians as to whether or not Rahab listed in Matthew is the same Rahab as this one in Joshua. Jewish tradition identifies Rahab as marrying Joshua, the leader of the Israelites; yet there is no Joshua as husband of Rahab in Matthew. Other scholars see this as a case of Matthew using literary license (common at the time) in skipping a few generations in his account in Matthew, and this may be some other Rahab. For this study, we are embracing this Rahab as *the* Rahab, great-great-(however many greats) grandmother of David, because this Rahab was instrumental in making a way for Jesus' birth one day, just as that Matthew 1 genealogy tells us.

Read Rahab's story in Joshua 2:1-11 and Matthew 1:3-5.

What had the spies done?

Who was interested in the spies' activities?

Where did Rahab hide the men?

What report could the men take back to Joshua?

Rahab was named a prostitute in the account of the spies. Some say the men went to visit her because a brothel would be a good place to obtain information; others rebut that no information was sought there according to the passage. Still others state that Rahab may have been a simple innkeeper and not of ill repute at all, or that the men only sought a bed and information, nothing more. We know that she is called "prostitute" several times in this passage, as well as twice in the New Testament. Even with all the unknowns, this is a pivotal point of the Israelite story, entering the promised land and conquering with God's blessing. Rahab as prostitute is a powerful message of how God loves people despite their reputation or past.

As a prostitute, politician, or pious person, God does not look at our past or our reputations when we come to him. He looks at our hearts. God can do more than just peek at our faces and see how we feel; he looks at our intentions, desires, fears, actions, reactions, joys, and sorrows. He understands the fullness of who we are and why we do the things we do. God wants to see that our hearts belong to him and that we seek him and do his will. Some quote Joshua 2:9-11 as Rahab's confession of faith.

Do you agree, and why or why not?

Rahab found herself with a problem when the king's messengers arrived at her door. She needed to get rid of them without causing problems for herself. She was stuck between giving up the men of God and getting rid of the soldiers any way possible, even lying.

Do you agree with her choice of lying to the men? Why or why not?

Rahab's Hope

We know little of Rahab. She was also from the land of Canaan (like Tamar). We are not told how she came to be a prostitute, but perhaps came to it as a last resort to take care of herself and her family. Rahab lived on the margins culturally, just like the literal placement of her home on the edges of the city. She perhaps was sneered at in the streets by the wives of her clients. I can only imagine that she was alone and marginalized, with companionship only in her house with family and staff.

If we assume verses 9-11 are Rahab's profession of faith in God, then we see that Rahab's hope was for a different life. She hoped to be released from the bondage of prostitution and brought into the Israelite clan. She may have hoped for the life of a simple washer woman, a flax farmer, or a patron and mother; we cannot see exactly what life she hoped for. We can see that she hoped in God, in whom she had faith. She told of the certainty of who God was and chose him.

Rahab's hope led to her faith; she was confident in what she hoped for. She was confident God would conquer her town and she hoped for life with him.

> On Week 1, Day 1, you noted a current hope. Take a moment now to consider the faith that you have, the confidence that God will act on that hope. Write a profession of faith that this hope will come to be.

Issue

Week 2, Day 2 Rahab

Rahab hid the Israelite spies on the roof and deceived the king's men by telling them the spies had left at nightfall, even including the direction the men supposedly had gone. She was in hot water, as lying to a king would certainly get her in trouble.

Rahab told the spies that the residents of Jericho, herself included, heard of how the Israelites had crossed the Red Sea on dry land and destroyed two kings and their hearts melted in fear. The Red Sea miracle had happened forty years before, when the Israelites left Egypt, yet the people still remembered and noted that the God of the Israelites was strong. The inhabitants of the city understood the threat to their lives.

Read Rahab's story in Joshua 2:8-16. As you read, note the following questions:

What did Rahab ask of the spies?

How did Rahab get the spies out of the city?

Rahab faced one threat to her life as she and the others in the city saw they were in the sights of the Israelites. She faced another threat when she lied to the king's messengers—likely putting her life and the lives of those who worked with her or her family at risk. She needed to eliminate these threats. She had an issue to handle: what to do with these spies.

Her understanding of who these men were and the danger they posed to herself, her business, her family, and even her city-state provided her with the insight to identify the problem before it happened and find a solution.

I'm not sure that I would consider hiding men in drying flax, given that flax is a tall grass-like plant. It looks like wheat if you are familiar with it. To dry such thin stalks, it would need to be laid out and turned regularly. Flax would not be stacked like hay into large piles, so to consider hiding men in the flax sounds ridiculous. Yet, the solution she came up with did work. She used what was at hand to solve the problem at hand.

Her solution may be rather unglamorous—dried flax on her rooftop is hardly a James Bond kind of disguise. She began her day like any other, perhaps making breakfast, hanging out the laundry and washing the dishes, turning the flax to let it dry. And in the ordinary things that she had at hand, she found a place to temporarily address one of the threats to her life. By hiding the men, she kept them out of sight of the king's messengers and clear from consequences of lying.

It was on an ordinary day when she first met the men who complicated everything. It is often in the ordinary that we meet God as well. Most of our days are spent in the usual ways, and solutions come through what surrounds us just as Rahab's solution came among the quite ordinary drying flax.

> Name some recent solutions you created for common problems at work, at home, or in a relationship.

When I consider my walk with Christ, there have been important moments, high and low, but most of my growth has been in the daily or ordinary. The daily practice of seeking God has brought the most growth. This day for Rahab was likely an exciting one, but it started with putting her pants on (figuratively) one leg at a time and ended with pulling the covers up to shield her in the night. Yet, in this ordinary day, she met God, served him, and served others.

God is certainly at the big event like the wedding, but he dwells in the marriage. His coming is envisioned at Christmas, but he lives in us all year. Special moments occur, but the special moments are not the only growth moments. Much of our growth happens when we aren't looking because it is in the ordinary. Growth occurs when we spend daily quiet time seeking the Lord in prayer and his Word. When we reach out to friends and have coffee or share a meal. When we are wiping noses and snapping car seats. When we are mediating disagreements, replying to emails, and sitting in meetings. When we are driving to softball practice or the company picnic. When we sign documents and approve requests. These daily things do not exclude the Spirit. He is with us in these moments. And we grow. We thrive in the ordinary when we reach out and grasp hope as Rahab did.

What parts of your ordinary day lead to spiritual growth?

Action

Week 2, Day 3 Rahab

Rahab declared her faith, and in so doing, also expressed her hope in God by asking for mercy. She indicated that she knew not only God's strength but more of his character in that he was merciful. And she immediately began serving God by assisting the spies in leaving the city unseen. Then, Rahab had to wait.

Read more of Rahab's story by reading Joshua 2:17-24.

What did Rahab have to do to save herself and her family?

What conditions did the Israelites put on their response to Rahab?

Rahab hoped in God for a better future and for saved lives, so she obeyed his Word through his people. She lashed a scarlet cord to her window and had faith that was enough.

Her house must have had a front door as well, but she did not tie a scarlet cord to the front door, only to the window. She didn't need a signal to the Israelites in the streets to leave her house alone. She demonstrated faith—confidence in what she hoped for and assurance about what she could not see. She had faith that God was protecting her home and those inside it. That is faith: confident hope. I admit that I would have considered putting a scarlet cord at every entrance to the house, door or window, thinking that man would need the indicator if not God. Yet Rahab followed God's words and did not question the simplicity of such a plan.

Rahab was called upon to obey, not to question. What I mention of my thoughts of tying a string at every door or window, that was me "questioning" Rahab and the plan. But Rahab did not question or second-guess; she obeyed. She guided the men as they were leaving. They guided her with God's Word. God chose her to help the spies, but God sent the spies to help her as well; there was collaboration.

Our relationships, particularly with other believers, can be guiding like this. God sent Rahab to help the men and even strategize with them. She misdirected the king's men and then she advised the spies on where to go from the town, and how long to wait so they were not caught. They told her to tie a cord on one window and gather her loved ones to her home. I find myself considering the men and Rahab because they likely all experienced fear in this situation, yet they must have encouraged one another and set their minds on God.

Who has God sent to your life to guide and help you in your walk?

After this short time of encouragement, the spies left and returned to give their report to Joshua. Then the Israelites prepared to enter and take the land that God had promised them. The Israelites crossed over the Jordan River into the land of Canaan on dry land, which again melted the hearts of the Canaanites. They set up camp and prepared to siege Jericho. During these days of waiting, Rahab stood. She placed her hope in God and faithfully waited.

Her action was complete when she tied the cord and called her family to her in obedience. Then she had to stand in faith. There are times to act and times to believe. I admit I am not very good at waiting (perhaps you noticed when I wanted to tie a cord to every opening in the house). In Rahab's shoes, I think I would struggle. I may have opened the window and checked on the situation every hour of every day of that waiting, much to my family's consternation. Yet Rahab obeyed. She did it immediately, tying the one cord as soon as the men left.

> Describe a time that you have done as God instructed, then grabbed hold of hope and stood in faith, including any struggle in the waiting.

Our hopes may grow stronger or change altogether as we walk with God. Rahab experienced the fear, or reverence, of the Lord and hoped to see his goodness. We could say that is the overarching hope that she had: to see God's goodness in releasing her from prostitution and saving her family in the battle for Jericho. It is good to narrow our focus of hope, so that we pray for the particular things of our hearts with direction. God is always good, for example, but the good that he reveals in my life is different from that he revealed in Rahab's life. Rahab wanted to see God's goodness, but that was specifically to be saved with him forever, and to be saved from the Israelite's siege.

> Write a brief prayer specifying the goodness of God that you hope to see.

Blessing

Week 2, Day 4 Rahab

Rahab waited, but God was working. The Israelites were moving toward Jericho. The spies returned to Joshua and gave the report, then the nation crossed the river Jordan into the land that God had promised them forty years earlier. They took time to set up a memorial to praise God for the safe passage on dry ground, and they rededicated themselves to God through circumcision. They celebrated Passover, another safe passage that God had granted out of Egypt. Rahab waited. The estimate is that there were about two weeks between the time the spies left Rahab's house and when they returned to begin the siege.

> **Read** of the defeat of Jericho as Rahab's account continued in Joshua 6:1, 12-25 and in Hebrews 11:30-31.

How did the Israelites carry out the attack on Jericho?

What happened to Rahab and her family?

The wall crumbled, but she did not. She lashed a scarlet cord to her window and the walls crumbled around her and it seemed no one was the wiser about her traitorous behavior. She was literally rescued twice in just days—from the betrayal of her people (lying to the king) and from being killed by the falling rubble. I find it so cool that the second time her life was saved, trumpets were enough to fell walls.

Her family was saved, and she was brought to a new place. Rahab and her family were led outside of Jericho and the city was burned. This woman who had lived in the margins was brought into the Israelite clan. She was integrated into society, taken from Canaan to the clan of God's people. She chose to follow God, and he took her from prostitution and to a new life.

She was brought not only into his chosen people, but apparently into the lineage that brought us the Messiah. Rahab's past did not define her future. Rahab's hope in God defined her future, certain that God cared for her. God saw who she was, not who she had been. Her past, the time when God was not her focus and she fell short of his glory, was forgiven and removed from her as far as east is from west. God sees who we are today and has removed anything that we may have done before seeking him the same way.

God is ready to heal and forgive anything that you may carry from your past. Just as Rahab declared her faith in God, you too can do so and leave behind anything lingering from the past.

> Take a moment to draw an image that represents something you have left behind as you came to Christ or something you now choose to leave behind to follow Christ today.

Rahab's past did not define her; God valued Rahab. He valued her while she offered a roof to the spies, he valued her when he saved her life (twice!), he valued her when she was brought out to the Israelite camp, and he valued her as he brought her into belonging with his people and as he made her a mother. Rahab showed many characteristics God values. She was generous, bold, loving, responsible, humble, patient, and family oriented. She demonstrated hope and faith. She was not perfect (see lies above), but her heart was turned toward pleasing God.

Rahab married Salmon and stands in the line of Christ. God's work in Rahab's life showed the worth he placed on her, and that work had lasting ramifications. How much more we understand our worth to God when we see God's work in our own lives also has lasting ramifications!

He values you as well. He valued you before you knew him. He valued you when he saved you. He valued you when you began this study. He values you today. He values you like jewels of a crown.

Take a few minutes to consider the worth that God sees in you. List some of the characteristics that God gave you that are valuable.

Reflection

Week 2, Day 5 Rahab

Rahab was in a place where she knew of God and decided to have a personal relationship with him, accepting him by faith. She hoped for salvation from the invasion of her town, obeyed in hope, and walked in faith. She could not see how God would keep her and her family safe but chose to obediently tie a cord and expect God to act.

I mentioned that I would likely look out the window where the cord was tied every hour, wondering where the Israelites were. I would also surely imagine how they were planning to get me and my family out safely.

Would they come in the night and take us away unbeknownst to the city? Would they dig a hole under the wall and get us out? What would they do and how would they keep us safe? There was no way to see what they would do in advance. She waited in faith and not sight. It seems she did not check out the window every hour as I perhaps would have.

Remember that one of the original Hebrew words for hope, *qavah*, is "lying in wait." Lying in wait, like a lion tensed to pounce upon its prey, like the tension in a rubber band. Like that cord Rahab tied outside her window. She must have experienced great trepidation in placing a simple rope on her window. But her hope was not in a cord; it was in God. And she laid in wait for him to act—however that action may have looked.

God is the one that we hope in while we hope for a better or different future. A cord is a poor thing to hope in. But God is mighty to save.

Think again of what you are hoping for. Are you hoping in God's goodness and might or trusting in your own strength and skill?

What have you done, or could you do, to hand God the cord that you are holding?

RUTH

Context

Week 3, Day 1 Ruth

Ruth's story is one that spans an entire book of the Bible and is one of only two books named after a woman. Her story is set during the time of the judges. This was the time after conquering the promised land, but before the Israelites were ruled by kings. This approximately 500-year period of the judges was a time known for lawlessness and disobedience, a time marked by famine and suffering.

A family of four from the land of Judah, which means they had descended from Judah, had left their home in Bethlehem to escape a famine and settled in the land of Moab. It is into this family that Ruth married. That is the little we know of Ruth: She was a Moabite woman who lived in the time of the judges.

In a short time, the men in the family died, leaving three widows. Naomi, the mother, heard that the famine had ended in her hometown and decided to return. She prepared to leave and told her daughters-in-law to go back to their fathers. Ruth, however, was not willing to go back to her father's home and chose instead to accompany Naomi.

Read Ruth 1:1-18 and Matthew 1:5.

What do you gather about Ruth's character based on this reading?

In verses 16 and 17, Ruth presented her case for staying with Naomi. Name three commitments that Ruth made in these verses.

It would seem Naomi wanted the women to come with her, since she packed them up, and then it was as they were along the road that she actually sent them back. She perhaps wanted company and family close to her, but struggled with doubt that she had anything to offer them and changed her mind. Or perhaps Naomi faced the reality of the dangerous road when three women were traveling alone. So, Naomi offered the two women, Ruth and Orpah, the opportunity to return home to their fathers. This offer indicated that Naomi did not expect to be able to provide for the women. However, their fathers likely could care for them.

Yet Ruth seemed to accept the danger of the road and the possibility of little in Bethlehem when they arrived. She was prepared to leave her homeland and follow an older woman to an unknown land with unknown people. The "known" for Ruth was one woman and that particular woman's God. Ruth made the choice of the difficult road rather than going back to her father (where she would likely be cared for and marry again).

We have perhaps heard there are no guarantees in life, that even gravity may fail. Yet the hope that we have challenges all of those statements about nothing being certain in life. In Christ, we hope. In Christ, much is certain. He is certain. Ruth is a model of hoping in a person, God. And her certainty of a better life with him was so great that it transformed her unknown. Most of us have unknowns in our lives, from who we will marry to how we will make it to the end of the month.

Just as God was with Ruth in going toward the unknown, God is with us, and that can change the way we view our circumstances. What unknown are you facing or have you faced recently?

At times, we feel that everything is unknown, and it is easy to lose hope about the "when" or "how" these things will become known. We get frustrated or are fearful of the unknown. Yet, Ruth chose the unknown because she had God with her, and she hoped in him. Romans 5:5 says, *"And hope does not put us to shame, because God's love has been poured out into our hearts through the Holy Spirit, who has been given to us."* Our circumstances do not overwhelm us, our unknowns do not scare us, and we stand on his love, knowing hope will not disappoint us.

Consider the unknowns you faced in the past. It may have been a new school, a new job, a new city, a new task in your job, a new role as boss or spouse. Jot down the ways that you coped with those unknowns and what made you successful in facing them.

Ruth's Hope

We have Ruth's direct words to understand her hope in verses 16 and 17. She described the hope that she had as being with Naomi, her people, and her land. She also acknowledged God as her own. The hope that Ruth expressed was to continue to live in family with Naomi. She sought family and chose Naomi and God, a "found family" as they are often called in literature. She chose Naomi's people, land, and God, making them her hope.

Ruth faced the unknown, believing that what she could not see, and had not ever seen, was better than what she was leaving behind. She was leaving behind her family of origin, the possibility of marriage and being cared for, and she was looking toward an unknown land with a woman who basically admitted she could not care for Ruth. Yet Naomi also offered a life with God. That is hope!

She looked to something that was better—here, she only had God and Naomi to look to for that "better." She had two people who represented something better than her current circumstances. God too should be enough for us as we consider our present circumstances; knowing he is there makes it better.

God has many characteristics that strengthen our hope in him. Think back to those unknowns from the previous question. What characteristics of God were evident at that time?

Issues

Week 3, Day 2 Ruth

As Ruth accompanied Naomi on the road to Bethlehem; they may have travelled anywhere from thirty to sixty miles (48-96 kilometers), or up to ten days to get there by foot. A person standing in Bethlehem could look to the land of Moab, on the opposite shore of the Dead Sea. As the crow flies, it was not far, but they had to go around the sea and cross the Jordan. They were greeted by the community upon arrival and settled on the land that Naomi's husband had left behind.

Read Ruth 1:19-3:1.

What do you understand Naomi's feelings were when they arrived in Bethlehem?

What title did Boaz give Ruth in their interaction?

What reason did Boaz give for his kindness to Ruth?

How did Naomi respond as Ruth recounted her day?

Ruth came to this new land and took on the responsibility of caring for her mother-in-law; this much we are told. Given the information shared about Naomi, I imagine Ruth also took care of the house, prepared the meals, and saw to what little there may have been in the farmland surrounding the house where they stayed. She may have had to wake and tend to Naomi as well if her depression and age were as advanced as it seemed.

Ruth was a constant strength to her mother-in-law. Perhaps this is what Boaz refers to when he says to Ruth, *"I have been told all about what you have done for your mother-in-law"* (2:11), that kindness must be the care she has for Naomi, as we are told nothing else. She is strong and kind in her actions. Many who care for families on their own can become bitter and unkind, but Ruth shines in this characteristic.

It is not a "problem" when we are caregivers, however it can be a weight to carry the responsibility for the care of others, big and small. Ruth seems to be the one who went out to gather in the fields and perhaps Naomi was tending the home. What I see is that Naomi was depressed upon her return to Bethlehem and may have been weary from the voyage, doing less than Ruth in the home. Her depression and age may have made it challenging to contribute to the physical work of the home. Ruth would have perhaps borne the weight of caring for a dependent. Caring for young or old, spouse or parent or sibling, can add a weight of great responsibility to our lives.

If you are a caregiver, consider two people you have a relationship with that you can lean on for support in dealing with this stress. If you do not have these kinds of relationships, list one person you may try to develop such a relationship with.

If you are not a caregiver right now, consider those who are caregivers in your life (perhaps to others) and write down two things you can do for them to support them.

What we see in the final verse for today is that Naomi had a motherly role toward Ruth. No matter the age of those we care for, there is always a blessing and a relationship that balances that weight with joy. Naomi wanted to provide for her daughter-in-law long-term, or perhaps at least better than the situation in which they were living. She sought a family for Ruth, a husband.

In a certain sense, I look at this and see an issue, a momma sticking her nose into daughter's business. But most of us would say that the issue for Naomi is not busybody-ness but rather how to ensure care for Ruth long-term. The loving mother-daughter relationship of caring for one another identified the issue of long-term care. So, we have two issues that the ladies show us: weight of caregiving and long-term provision.

Hidden strength often comes out when we interact with others. Sometimes it is not in a caregiving way, but a cooperative way of interacting with others. Naomi and Ruth had this mutual relationship that offers strength to each other.

Consider three or four interactions with others over the last week or two. How would you categorize those interactions (challenging, encouraging, arguments, caregiving, etc.)?

Which of your strengths were apparent in those interactions?

Action

Week 3, Day 3 Ruth

At the end of Ruth 1, we find that Ruth and Naomi arrived around the time of the barley harvest, and Ruth went out to gather and process the grain. That would have been in April. At the end of the second chapter, Ruth worked through the wheat and barley harvests, which would have been in May. We read in Chapter 3 that Bethlehem was in the middle of another barley harvest, which means a year or more may have passed by this time. We considered two issues that Ruth was dealing with: the weight of being a caregiver and her own long-term care, as the two were alone to provide for each other, though poor and widowed.

Read Ruth 3:1-18.

Describe the plan that Naomi shared with Ruth.

Ruth said that she "will do whatever you [Naomi] say" (v. 5). How did Ruth stray from the instructions?

How did Boaz respond to being woken in the night?

What did Ruth ask of Boaz, and what was his response?

This chapter provides an interesting scenario to address the issues that Ruth was facing. It is good to remember, though, that God provided for the widows and orphans, that day and long term. In Leviticus 19:9-10 and Deuteronomy 24:19-21, God commanded the Israelites to leave the corners of fields unharvested, and any straw which fell was to be left uncollected. These portions left behind were designated for the poor, widowed, orphans, and foreigners who worked the fields to gather the foodstuffs. This must have been a relief to the women to know that some food would be available to harvest. God cared for the women's burden.

Boaz was an upright man and insisted that Ruth gather grain in his fields as provided for under these instructions from God. Boaz was God's conduit for this provision; during the time of the judges, people were not inclined to follow God's law. In Chapter 2, after just one day of work, Ruth had an ephah, or thirty pounds (thirteen kilograms) of grain to carry home. This is the equivalent of carrying the weight of four gallons (sixteen liters) of water home! Her shawl was overflowing. Ruth received such a blessing by working in Boaz's fields, according to God's provision and faithfulness.

Our hope rests in God and holds firm when we stand on his faithfulness. The ladies had survived for a full year (or more) on God's faithfulness in providing for them. Draw a timeline of your own life and mark it with times when God acted in faithfulness to you.

The women were cared for under God's law, but Ruth began to hope for a better situation for herself and Naomi, to have a home and to be *"well provided for"* (3:1, 5). Naomi understood the law, the culture, and the people of the land and was able to guide Ruth in realizing this hope. Naomi explained to Ruth that she should wait until the men had finished their work, *then* approach Boaz. The work during the harvest was often completed late in the evening as it kept the progress hidden from thieves. During the lawless time of the judges, the workers and owner slept nearby to protect the harvest.

We need to address the issues that come up with the instruction that Naomi gave Ruth. It all sounds a little scandalous. Naomi told Ruth to go to Boaz in the dead of night, ensuring that no one saw her. It might sound like Naomi is saying to Ruth to go and offer herself. However, most scholars and commentaries agree this is not an indication of sex.[3]

The threshing floor at that time of night, with the workers around, was a public area. Boaz went to sleep, and Ruth approached him and uncovered his feet. Some have indicated that "feet" is a euphemism; however, the Hebrew word is only used one other time in Scripture and refers to arms and legs or extremities.[4] It seems the intention of uncovering his feet was simply to wake him as he would get chilled in the spring night. So, Ruth uncovered his feet and laid there. By laying at his feet, she placed herself in a submissive or servant position, not the position of a wife beside him.

> The scenario put Ruth's reputation at risk. This must have been calculated by Naomi and Ruth. Do you agree with risking Ruth's reputation by approaching Boaz at night? Why or why not?

We should acknowledge that it is dark or secluded, and their reputations may have been tarnished during this one evening. Naomi and Ruth calculated the risk, and it was by knowing Boaz was upstanding that they decided it was worth it. We can be certain it was not an intimate encounter as we see the upright character that both had demonstrated through the story. The gossip about Ruth, as mentioned in Chapter 2, was that she was in good standing with the community for all she'd done for Naomi. Boaz had extended grace and protection to her at each turn.

As Boaz woke, Ruth called herself a servant and requested that Boaz *"spread the corner of your garment over me,"* (3:9). The word translated as "garment" is the same word that appeared in Boaz's blessing of Ruth in 2:12 translated as "wing." Ruth requested the formal protection of Boaz, or more specifically, marriage. With this proposal, there was no intention to move it to consummation, nor was it taken by Boaz in that way. In response, Boaz said, *"The Lord bless you, my daughter,"* (3:10) and says she has shown kindness. The titles used—daughter and servant—as well as the reputation each had supports the interpreted lack of any sexual encounter on the threshing floor. The word "wing" or "cover" was not a sexual inuendo, but a way indicating protection.

Boaz honored Ruth; however, he stated that another had precedence as the kinsman-redeemer. He affirmed he would pursue a solution, as Ruth suggested. Sending Ruth away into the streets at midnight would have been a terrible disservice to her after agreeing to try to provide for Ruth and Naomi long-term. Walking home alone in the dark during the time of the judges would have put Ruth at risk of harm or death.[5] So, Ruth was invited to remain along with the workers on the threshing floor. We again see protection offered rather than sexual opportunity.

By the time the workers woke, Ruth had already gone home. The risk to her reputation and the risk to her person had to be balanced, and they apparently succeeded in protecting it. As the sun was just coming up, the men were sleeping, and the streets were only beginning to wake for polite society, Ruth made her way to Naomi to tell of her time talking with Boaz.

Ruth had assistance from Naomi and then accepted assistance from Boaz as well. Ruth was not able to do more than approach Boaz; she had to leave her hope in someone else's hands. Boaz took Ruth's hopes in his hands and helped, seeking to respond to the future Ruth envisioned. He immediately took the issues to the city gate and reminded the guardian-redeemer of his options.

Describe a time when you found that issues were only resolved once help was involved.

Blessing

Week 3, Day 4 Ruth

In Chapter 3, we found that Ruth took risks and proposed marriage to Boaz, but he said he was not able to accept right away. There was another who was a closer guardian-redeemer, also called "kinsman-redeemer." The concept of redeeming a kinsman is laid out in Leviticus 25:25-55 and says that the nearest family member (kinsman) was obliged to step in to buy the land of those who fell on hard times. The law extended to buying back land if it had been sold to those outside their tribe, as well as buying back those who had sold themselves or family into slavery to survive. It was common practice for those who became poor to sell their land and possessions and sometimes even themselves and their families to pay debts or to survive.

Read of this kinsman-redeemer in Ruth 4:1-22.

Boaz split his invitation to the closer guardian-redeemer into two parts. What did each part consist of?

What was the blessing of the elders at the gate upon Boaz's announcement?

How did the women bless Naomi upon the birth of Obed?

Chapter 1 opened with Ruth choosing Naomi, her God, her land, and her people. The final chapter ends with Ruth being claimed by God and the people and having a son who would own the land and was considered heir. Ruth's faithfulness to God and his priorities brought great blessings to her, fulfilling her every hope.

Ruth was blessed in marrying a godly man who carried out God's laws in his heart and not just to the letter. She was then blessed by expanding her family from Naomi to a husband, then a child. This baby was called the guardian-redeemer of Naomi and even called her son, as the nearest relative and heir to her husband and son's property. The blessings that Ruth received in the realization of her hope went on to bless others.

Blessings have this remarkable uncountability to them. We note that Ruth was blessed by the marriage to Boaz. However, we also see the blessing extended to Naomi, in having an heir, and Boaz, in having a child and a godly wife, and in this case the blessing continued through the line of David on to the birth of Jesus. How could we possibly count the blessings in this one account! The blessing that Ruth received was neither diminished nor divided, though it passed on to others. We may say that it was multiplied to others or shared. A blessing is not limited to one—not one person or family, not one moment or time period. When God blesses us, it doesn't mean that there are fewer blessings available for others, or that a blessing for me is one less blessing for you. Blessings are simply uncountable.

How has God blessed you in the last six months? How has that blessing also been of benefit to others?

When Boaz was at the gate and completed his business, the elders blessed Boaz and Ruth. They prayed that God would bless the family with fruitfulness building up the family of Israel and that they would have standing in Bethlehem. The women as well blessed the child, that he would be famous and renew Naomi in old age. These prayers were about their current life, yet we can see that they looked to the past to see the blessings upon the tribe of Judah, their own family. These blessings also impacted the future still unknown to them.

Ruth was faithful to God and family and was a virtuous woman. Through her actions, she showed that her choice was for God and despite the difficulties and hard work, she was faithful to him. She held firmly to God in her difficulties. Ruth lived on the generosity of others; she was very poor and surely struggled to make ends meet. Yet, she held to her *"hope as an anchor for the soul, firm and secure"* (Hebrews 6:19). God is our hope. He is faithful through all.

God blessed her through the choices she made and the actions she undertook. Faithfulness is about holding on to God no matter the circumstances. When our circumstances rage around us, when the difficulties come, we need only hold to the anchor of Christ to come through the storm.

> During this week, consider how God has been faithful to you.
> Jot down how he has shown his faithfulness.

Ruth married Boaz, integrating her into the people of Naomi that she had claimed as her own in Chapter 1. It brought her to the full realization of belonging to Naomi's God, land, and people. Then she was also blessed with a son.

Reflection

Week 3, Day 5 Ruth

God is always working for us. Ruth is a book that includes God's direct and indirect work throughout. It includes various blessings from God and from people, one to another. It shows us how God works in and through our lives. There are two instances in the book of Ruth where God was identified as having actively worked directly in the lives of those mentioned (Ruth 1:6; 4:13).

How do you expect God to interact with you? Be specific.

There are months and even years when we may say "I don't see God." Yet God is always working. He often works in the background, and how we wish he would only work in the light. He often brings together people and circumstances which can only be explained by his action and will. Ruth happened to work in Boaz's fields; he happened to be a righteous man. The closer kinsman-redeemer wasn't interested in marriage to Ruth. These circumstances all worked together to bring about the blessings that we saw in Ruth's life. God interacted with her through apparent "happenstance."

Ruth 1:6 and 4:13 both mention God's direct action, rather than behind the scenes, benefiting the people. In Chapter 1, God *"came to the aid of his people by providing food for them"*. Ruth was able to conceive because the Lord enabled it in Chapter 4. These direct actions are different from the circumstances that came about to assist in Ruth's life. It would not be such a leap to think that these two actions were prayed for. We are told so specifically in the blessings over Boaz and Ruth to be fruitful. During a drought, it is common for people to pray for relief. When we pray, we are more likely to be looking for God's actions, and attribute them to him. Whatever the circumstance, God is working.

God works in meaningful ways in the background of our lives as well as the foreground. It may be easier to see him in the crises of our lives, but we can see his work any time. We need only look for it, as we do when we pray for things.

> What is your longest-standing prayer to God? How has he worked in your life in response to that prayer?

We have the declaration of faith from Ruth in verses 1:16-17; we don't know how God spoke to her or what specifically brought her to faith. We may identify that God brought Naomi to her life as a key to prepare her heart for faith.

> Consider your own declaration of faith. How did God work in your life to bring it about?

BATHSHEBA

Context

Week 4, Day 1 Bathsheba

Bathsheba is introduced to us as a grown, married woman who lived after the time of judges, during the reign of the second king of Israel. She was the wife of Uriah, a Hittite, and was the daughter of Eliam. Both Bathsheba's father and husband were listed among the thirty mighty warriors of David (2 Samuel 23:34, 39). This would have meant that she grew up in a military family and married into one. She is the only of our study who is an Israelite woman, as her father, Eliam, is from Giloh in the land of Judah (Joshua 15:51).

Bathsheba is where we intersect with David, second king of Israel and one of Jesus' most famous ancestors. At the time when Bathsheba came to David's attention, he was already a well-established king and sat on his throne in Jerusalem. It was springtime, and when most kings went out to war, David sent his warriors out to defeat the Ammonites, but he remained home.

Read 2 Samuel 11; 12:15-20, 24-25 and Matthew 1:6

How did Bathsheba become pregnant?

What did she do when she found she was pregnant?

What became of their relationship by the end of the reading?

In the cultural norms of the time, a full bathroom was traditionally set up on the rooftops of Jerusalem. This means there were curtains or rugs hung around the bath and Bathsheba was likely never uncovered in public view. However, the palace may have been a much grander, and taller, building than those around it, and it could be that the palace, and David, had an extensive view over (literally) all of the town. In this passage, we can see that there was an imbalance of power in play. David was king while Bathsheba was the wife of a soldier.

Verse 3 helps us understand that David knew that he was calling on a married woman who was from a family of importance to his reign, related to his thirty mighty warriors. Second Samuel 11:4 says he called her to the palace, he slept with her, *"then she went back home"*. This account reminds us all too well of stories of powerful people who have taken advantage of those around them. Bathsheba was made a victim, raped with no voice or choice in the act. She obeyed her king by following the summons and was powerless to reject his advances; her king used his power to get what he wanted from her.

In 2 Samuel 12, we find that God responded to this rape and sent Nathan, David's prophet, to point out the sin and abuse of power. It may have seemed that Bathsheba was alone when she was victimized, but God saw it all and corrected David for his behavior. God was with Bathsheba and stood up for her.

So often we find ourselves in unexpected and uncomfortable situations, and we lean only on ourselves, but God has not placed us here to be on our own. We are placed here to be part of fellowship, with others and with God. God sent his prophet Nathan, who rebuked David and made it clear that his abuse of power was displeasing to God. Nathan stood up for Bathsheba, and God was on Bathsheba's side.

> Who do you have in your corner when you find yourself in an unexpected situation?

> If you struggle to name a couple of people, identify one person you can approach and get to know better so that you will have someone to lean on in the future.

Bathsheba's Hope

Bathsheba demonstrates her hope to us through these passages. She was a woman who would have been identified as an adulterer when her pregnancy began to show. Her husband was at war, so it would have been clear that she had engaged in extra-marital sex. What was done in hiding would come to light. According to Deuteronomy 22:22 and Leviticus 20:10, a death sentence was placed on both the man and woman caught in adultery. Bathsheba had to reach out to the king to see how she could save herself and protect her child. By reaching out to this man of power, she shows us that she hopes to raise the child and protect him.

We are not told how long Bathsheba was married to Uriah, but we understand that the union created no children. This may have been a hope that she had for some time. Second Samuel 12:24 also tells us that she had another child with David, named Solomon. It seems that she hoped to be a mother and keep her children protected by her side.

Issue

Week 4, Day 2 Bathsheba

When Bathsheba married David, she joined a large extended family. According to 1 Chronicles 3:5, David and Bathsheba had four sons. However, Bathsheba was not David's only wife. He had children through other wives and concubines, as many as nineteen sons and one daughter are named in the Bible. Adonijah, whose mother was Haggith, was the oldest of David's living sons. As David grew older and was unable to rise from his bed any longer, Adonijah gathered a group of advisors to set himself up as king.

Read 1 Chronicles 22:5-10 and 1 Kings 1:1, 5-12.

David made an announcement about two things in the passage from 1 Chronicles. What were they?

Adonijah invited people to join his move to ascend to the throne of David in 1 Kings. Who stood by him and who refused?

The passage from 1 Chronicles 22 showed an active David who appointed his successor and prepared for the building of the temple of the Lord. Bathsheba must have been so proud to know that her son had been chosen above the others to be David's successor and the constructor of the temple. However, Bathsheba may have also been concerned about jealousy in the family and kept extra watch over him to protect him.

About nine years after the announcement that her son would become king[6], a threat arose to Bathsheba's son; David had become weak and one of his other sons wanted the throne. Adonijah, who was spoiled and had never been rebuked by his father, was aiming for the throne. Adonijah, a member of the royal family, would have been privy to the information that David shared in his announcements in 1 Chronicles. Yet, he set himself against God's word as given at that time by gathering officials and family around him and declared himself king, leaving Solomon and Bathsheba out of the coronation.

Disobedience to God is the root of much conflict. Bathsheba married into a family rife with conflict; there were rapes, murders, rivalries, and power plays. Each one was explicitly condemned in the Word of God. Now the disobedience to God had come to Bathsheba's door.

> Consider the impact of loved ones who have made choices to disobey God. How has that impacted your own life?

We have arrived at the point of the story where there was a weakened king and a conspiracy for the throne. This was a political mess which could lead to Solomon's death. Bathsheba had already lost one child, and her hope was to save and support her children. Her concern must have grown immensely, perhaps into desperation. Bathsheba was likely fearful for Solomon's life and under a great amount of stress given the political mess.

Consider the last time you were desperate for help. What caused your fear?

Bathsheba was not left alone in her desperation or anxiety. In 1 Chronicles 22:9-10, she was given God's promise for her son's reign and that it would be peaceful. She could stand on the promise of God. She also had a confidant, Nathan, who came to her to help. God's promises are for us and are good because he is good and cares for us (Matthew 6:25-34). He will never leave us nor forsake us, and he encourages fellowship with others to support us in our trials (Hebrews 10:24-25). Both God and Nathan were with Bathsheba in this difficulty. God is with you as well and you can stand on his promises, too.

Action

Week 4, Day 3 Bathsheba

Bathsheba hoped the best for her children, yet found herself in a situation where she and her child were threatened. Her motherly love was putting her at risk, but she focused on her children and had God on her side with the prophet, Nathan, assisting.

Read 1 Kings 1:11-40.

Who advised Bathsheba how to save Solomon, and what was the plan?

What did David do to intervene?

Who supported Solomon's appointment as ruler and what were their positions?

Nathan was a powerful and godly man. Yet he sought Bathsheba to initiate a bold challenge to the king. Given that he approached Bathsheba and not David directly, she may have had a role as advisor, perhaps behind the scenes. This would indicate that she had a positive relationship with David and potentially one of power, though she lived in a patriarchal society. Her status as woman did not keep her from being involved and influencing the happenings of the kingdom. Despite the influence that she apparently had, she still needed support to save her son. We see her interacting with more people and fighting for her son's best interest, perhaps the kingdom's best interest as well. I think what we see is the mama bear caring for her cub, too.

Bathsheba had no fear entering to see David, nor did she hesitate to boldly claim the promise that David had made regarding Solomon. David had given his word to Bathsheba, and she brought it back to mind to help in keeping her hope. And David, the earthly king, responded. How much more will God respond to our bold approach to his throne! God's promises are that much stronger as he is faithful (Deuteronomy 7:9; 1 Corinthians 1:9). We too can be bold and claim the promises of God, asking him to fulfill them as he is mighty to save (Zephaniah 3:17).

In your prayers, have you called out to God and stated his promises, asking for him to fulfill them? Jot those requests here.

What was the response?

God is powerful to respond to our situations, and he often works with us, but sometimes there is nothing for us to do as God works with and through others. Bathsheba talked to someone directly involved in the situation, and then she apparently stayed at the palace and was not at the anointing of her son as king. Bathsheba had hope to support her son, something that she herself could only work toward in part, God and others had to do the rest for her. Benaiah the head bodyguard would have to protect Solomon in her stead. Nathan and Zadok would support her son while she waited at the palace.

However much Bathsheba may have wanted to act herself, she could not save or protect Solomon on her own. She had enough power or influence to "get the ball rolling," so to speak. Then she had to step back and let God work through others. Firstly, David was engaged, even though he had apparently been a lax king of late. There were three others that David called on to realize the hope that Bathsheba held. She may have gone to the rooftop to look out on the people and city as Solomon went through the streets on the king's mule, watching for the safety of her child and that he would become king. It was something that she could not do on her own. She had to wait for God to work in and through others.

When we wait for God to work in and through others, it is important to remember that our hope is in Christ, not other people. We know that ultimately it is God who works things for our good and his glory; it is not our own activities that do so. Bathsheba did not hope in David, who had been bedridden and unaware of the goings-on in the kingdom. Nor did she hope in Benaiah, the bodyguard who was one person against Adonijah and his gathered cohorts. Nor could she hope in the priest or prophet to do anything more than pour oil. Her hope endured to support and protect Solomon, even as she waited for others to keep him safe in and through the power and will of God.

Consider how others may help realize your hope. How could you approach them or request their assistance?

She boldly challenged the king, but in so doing, she engaged heaven's armies to ensure things would be as God willed and she hoped.

Blessing

Week 4, Day 4 Bathsheba

Bathsheba's hope was to save and support her children. She saw threats to them and acted in faith that they would be well. She is perhaps the one woman in this study who does not fully see her hope realized while on earth, as she lost her first child seven days after his birth. Perhaps she hoped to see him again one day. However, we see that loss and grief did not stop her from hoping again. She had more children and continued to hope for their salvation and supporting them.

Read 1 Kings 2:13-25.

What did Adonijah ask of Bathsheba when he went to her?

How did she respond to the request?

How did Solomon respond to the request?

Bathsheba was blessed to have influence to help her children even after David's death. She was still in a powerful position where she could support her children. Adonijah sought her as a confidant to King Solomon, having approached her saying that Solomon would not deny her anything.

Much as Adonijah's attempt for the throne was based on ancient Near East tradition, and not God's will, he again tried to claim ancient Near East rights to the throne by asking for that which belonged to the former king. Bathsheba knew the traditions that called for a new king to care for the previous king's family, and renouncing any of the property of the previous king would have implied giving up some portion of power as well. Essentially, by asking for Abishag to be his wife, Adonijah asked Solomon for the right to challenge his throne. Bathsheba likely had two choices: deal with it herself or take it to Solomon.

In Bathsheba's shoes, would you have taken care of the issue yourself, or taken it to Solomon? Why?

If she dealt with it herself by refusing to take the request to her son, she was probably limited to only refusing. That would mean that the threat to her son would remain. She instead opted for the second and took the request to Solomon, who also saw that it was a threat and that Adonijah had violated his oath to support Solomon's reign.

The violation of the oath allowed Solomon just cause to execute Adonijah and therefore eliminate the threat to his reign. Bathsheba was clever in bringing the issue to the king to resolve. Her influence allowed for the removal of the challenge to her son through justice rather than revenge or any other means. She was blessed to see justice come to her son and the threat to his life removed through Adonijah's actions and not pettiness or additional bodily threat.

Bathsheba was blessed with a good relationship with her son. When Bathsheba brought the request to Solomon, his response was to get up from his throne and greet her personally, then call for a throne for her to be placed beside him for her. She was elevated as the queen-mother and made to sit beside her son, where she could advise him and support him all the days.

Bathsheba was blessed to be put in a position to continue to influence her children's welfare and to protect them. She was also blessed in seeing justice come to a threat to her son. Her hope was realized in that she was in a power position where she could begin to act on these things herself, sitting at the king's right hand.

Jesus sits at God's right hand, desiring to see you well, to sit beside you and within, and advise you to save you and support you. He is faithful to do so, ready to attend to you and your needs. He works for our good all the time. Bathsheba would only be a shadow of the advisor we have in Christ.

Imagine sitting together with Jesus, your advisor, and asking for what you need from him in the way of support and saving. Write a short prayer of hope below asking for his assistance; he is faithful to respond.

Reflection

Week 4, Day 5 Bathsheba

Bathsheba saw justice in the situation with Adonijah asking for Abishag to become his wife, just as in earlier years she saw God's justice in the rebuke of David over his actions toward her.

Justice in the Bible is not a set of rules or a judge who presides over a case or situation, it is fundamentally *to make something right*. God's justice is both punishing and restorative in order to make things right. When justice is required, one party is generally punished, and the other is restored; it takes two halves to bring about biblical justice.

This scene provides us a glimpse of God's justice: Adonijah is punished for having sinned against God and having sought the throne for himself while having at the same time recognized or elevated Bathsheba to a position of influence and honor after having been a victim of abuse of power.

Bathsheba was justly elevated after being a rape victim and was now able to protect a woman from being forced into marriage. Adonijah was ultimately punished not only by losing the throne he wanted, but because he broke his own vow to support Solomon's reign, he signed his own death warrant.

Consider injustice as you have seen it in your life. Choose one personal and one social injustice. Describe the punitive and restorative justice that God has brought or could bring to those two situations.

Jesus is the ultimate example of God's justice in both punishing him for our sins while simultaneously making it possible for each of us to be reunited with God. By paying for our sins, Jesus carried out the punitive part of justice. He also restored us to right relationship with God, thereby fulfilling the second part of justice. His one act on the cross bridged the gap of sin that had been created between us and God. God is of justice and love.

Jesus' one act made it impossible for anything to separate us from him. Use the space below to thank God for his justice in placing punishment on Christ and righteousness and restoration on you.

Jesus' ultimate act on earth affirms that he cares for us and works for our good. We do well to place our hope in him who is our anchor in the storms and injustices of life.

Conclusion

The examples within these four women who longed for righteousness and goodness in their lives shows us a future through hope. I don't think that any of them envisioned it in the way it actually unfolded. I think they would have all planned something different for themselves in the way their hopes were realized.

But hoping in God is not about how our hopes are realized, it is in the knowing—knowing God has our best at heart, no matter how it comes about. That is the very definition of hope: surety in the unseen. We do not see the how, but only God in the midst, God in the result.

Tamar. Rahab. Ruth. Bathsheba.

Tamar hoped for restoration in family, Rahab hoped to save her family, Ruth hoped to serve God and Naomi, and Bathsheba hoped to see her son safely on the throne, and all of them left a legacy of the strength of hope in the life of those who believe. They made far-reaching impacts even to today, as we read their stories. They hoped for more than their current circumstances and placed God at the center.

> Consider your own life and the changes that unpreferable circumstances have wrought. How has your hope led you to act in bold ways through faith like these women?

How has God blessed you through the work of hope in your life?

• • • ● • ● • • •

It is my prayer that you have been blessed by this study. To help others find this resource and multiply the blessing, please consider leaving a review.

Review Hope

Hope Study Resources

A small group study guide is available as a free download to subscribers of InspiritEncourage newsletters. Download this resources to use it with your small group today.

*Download Free
Guide*

Also By Sarah K. Howley

Women of the Old Testament Bible Studies
Hope: A Bible Study of Women in Jesus' Lineage
Faith (coming 2024)
Love (coming 2024)

Alive Again Bible Study on Forgiveness
Alive Again: Find Healing in in Forgiveness
Alive Again Bible Study: Find Healing in Forgiveness
Alive Again Forgiveness Prayer Journal

The Son Reveals the Father
I Am: An 8-Session Study of John
Heart: A 12-Session Study of Luke
Word: An 11-Session Study of Matthew
King: An 8-Session Study of Mark

About the Author

Sarah K. Howley is a Bible teacher, passionate about helping believers grow spiritually and take on the character of Christ. She is the founder of InspiritEncourage, an author, speaker, and trained Christian counselor. She has lived in over five countries on four continents and takes her own espresso wherever she goes. Sarah and her husband support initiatives for feeding the hungry and for expanding access to reading.

You can find Sarah on Facebook and Instagram @inspiritencourage. To book Sarah as a speaker at your next event, please contact her through her website. For weekly encouragement and information on her latest releases, sign up for Sarah's newsletter at InspiritEncourage.com.

Inspiri-
tEn-
courage

Endnotes

Week 1: Tamar

1. Judith Baskin, "Jewish Practices & Rituals: Covering of the Head," Jewish Virtual Library, Accessed November 16, 2023, https://www.jewishvirtuallibrary.org/covering-of-the-head.

2. Dina Khadr, "The Veil in Egypt and Beyond: A Brief History on the Practice and Its Symbolism Today," Egyptian Streets, Accessed November 16, 2023, https://egyptianstreets.com/2023/04/19/the-veil-in-egypt-and-beyond-a-brief-history-on-the-practice-and-its-symbolism-today/.
Red Lips High Heels – Gender in the Middle East, "The Veil in Ancient Middle Eastern/Western Asian Cultures," Accessed November 16, 2023, https://redlipshighheels.com/the-veil-in-ancient-middle-easternwestern-asian-cultures/.

Week 3: Ruth

3. Precept Austin, "Ruth 3:4-7 Commentary," Accessed November 8, 2023, https://www.preceptaustin.org/ruth_34-7.

4. John Piper, "Ruth: Strategic Righteousness," Desiring God, July 15, 1984, Accessed November 8, 2023, https://www.desiringgod.org/messages/ruth-strategic-righteousness.

5. https://www.biblegateway.com/passage/?search=ruth+3&version=NIV.
Precept Austin, "Ruth 3:13-15 Commentary," Accessed November 15, 2023, https://www.preceptaustin.org/ruth_313-18#3:13.

Week 4: Bathsheba

6. Bible Hub, "Bible Timeline," Accessed November 16, 2023, https://biblehub.com/timeline/.